Welcome, Baby!

A Gentle Conversation About Where Babies Come From for the Very Young Child

By Soyung Pak

Little Pond Books

First Printing, 2019

Cover and interior design by Sara Cramb

ISBN 978-1-7330255-1-5 (paperback)
ISBN 978-1-7330255-2-2 (ebook)

Published in the United States of America by Little Pond Books
Connect with us @littlepondbooks 🅕 🅣

Image Credits:
Front Cover: cucumber/Shutterstock.com (left), Africa Studio/Shutterstock.com (right)
Back Cover and Dedication Page: Eric Isselee/Shuttersock.com
Title Page: seasoning_17/Shutterstock.com

Interior Pages:
p. 4: anurakss/Shutterstock.com (top), smereka/Shutterstock.com (center), new-reporter/Shutterstock.com (bottom);
p. 5: Luis Louro/Shutterstock.com; p. 6: Brocreative/Shutterstock.com; p.7: Tiffany Bryant/Shutterstock.com;
p. 8: Dovzhykov Andriy/Shutterstock.com; p. 9: Hannamariah/Shutterstock.com (top), Tsekhmister/Shutterstock.com (bottom);
p. 10: Anton_Ivanov/Shutterstock.com (left), NoraphatPhotoss/Shutterstock.com (right); p. 11: Mike Truchon/Shutterstock.com (top left), Juris Kraulis/Shutterstock.com (top right), Andrea Izzotti/Shutterstock.com (bottom left), bluehand/Shutterstock (bottom right); p. 12: AnnekaShutterstock.com; p. 13: Sandy van Vuuren/Shutterstock.com (top), Nik Bruining/Shutterstock.com (bottom);
p. 14: Valeriy Velikov/Shutterstock.com; p. 15: Gelpi/Shutterstock.com; p. 16: Litvalifa/Shutterstock.com (top), Eric Isselee/Shutterstock.com (center), Africa Studio/Shutterstock.com (bottom); p. 17: Kasefoto/Shutterstock.com (top), Gelpi/Shutterstock.com (bottom left), Anurak Pongpatimet/Shutterstock.com (bottom right); p. 18: Inc/Shutterstock.com; p. 19: Inc/Shutterstock.com (left), Sebastian Kaulitzki/Shutterstock.com (right); p. 21: Jezper/Shutterstock.com; p. 22: Andrii Vodolazhskyi/Shutterstock.com (left and center), Rost9/Shutterstock.com (right); p. 23: Sebastian Kaulitzki/Shutterstock.com; p. 24: John Dory/Shutterstock.com;
p. 25: Ptaha I/Shutterstock.com (top left), Sebastian Kaulitzki/Shutterstock.com (top right, bottom left and bottom right);
p. 26: KonstantinChristian/Shutterstock.com (left), Martin Valigursky/Shutterstock.com (center), photomak/Shutterstock.com (right);
p. 27: MintImages/Shutterstock.com (top right), Raisman/Shutterstock.com (top left), HannaMonika/Shutterstock.com (bottom left), szefei/Shutterstock.com (bottom right); p. 28: sirtravelalot/Shutterstock.com

To Lucy, Anna and Julia

Birds that fly through the sky.

Animals that walk on land.

Sea life that swim in our waters.

And you.

And Me.

Every living creature on this planet has something in common.

We all need air and water and food to live.

But there is something else.

Can you guess?

We all started as an egg.

Did someone
say egg?

Yes,
an egg!

Not all eggs are the same.
Just like the life around us, eggs come in different sizes and shapes and colors.

An ostrich egg is large enough to be a soccer ball!

Blue bird eggs are blue like just like their feathers!

Clownfish eggs are so small it is hard to see them!

Look! These eggs are hatching!
These newborn animals are
opening their shells from the
inside and emerging into
the world.

Welcome
to the world,
chick!

Hello, baby crocodiles!

Greetings, little bugs!

But other babies don't hatch at all. The eggs of mammals transform and grow into babies inside their mothers.

What's a mammal?

Rabbits are mammals.

Horses are mammals.

Dogs are mammals.

If you have hair or fur, then you are probably a mammal.

17

Mammal eggs are so small that
you cannot see them.

To stay safe, mammal eggs stay
inside the mother in the womb,
a place near the mother's belly.

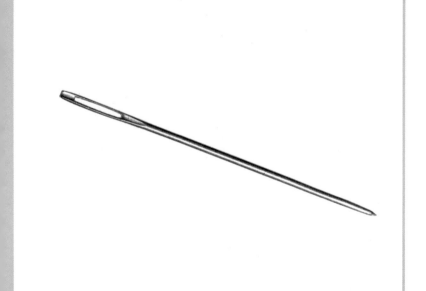

The human egg you
see here has been
magnified. Its true size
is smaller than the
head of a needle.
That's too small to see.

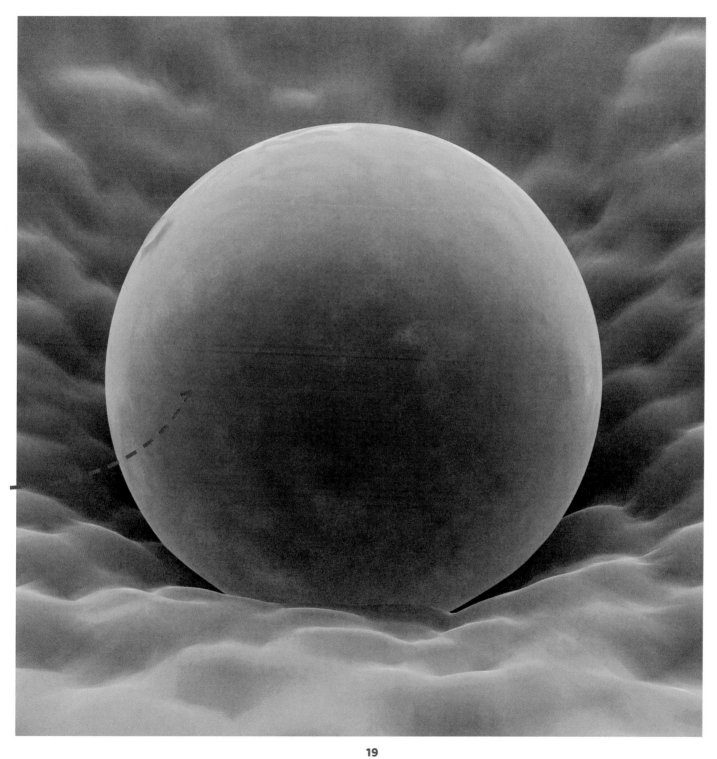

When an egg is joined by a
special cell called a sperm cell,
a miracle begins.

The egg can now become
a baby.

This is called fertilization.

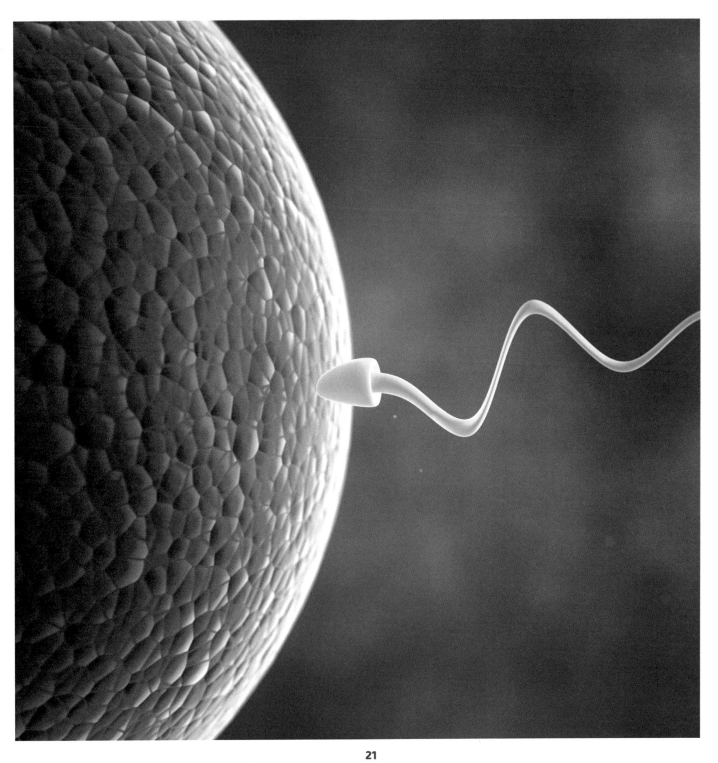

Once the egg is fertilized,
a change occurs.

The egg splits in two, then
divides and grows as it begins its
transformation...

 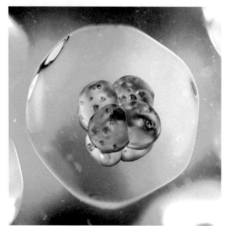 

...to become an embryo.

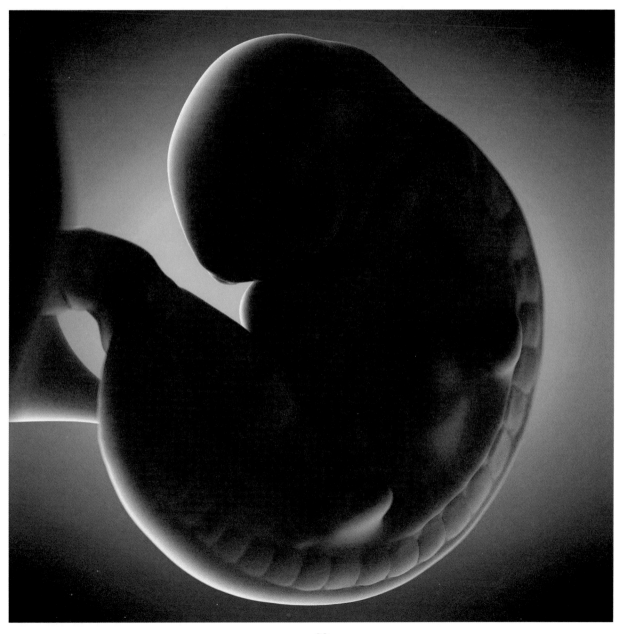

This is how YOU began!

For 40 weeks, you stayed inside the womb. In this protected place, eyes appeared, and hands, feet, fingers and toes grew.

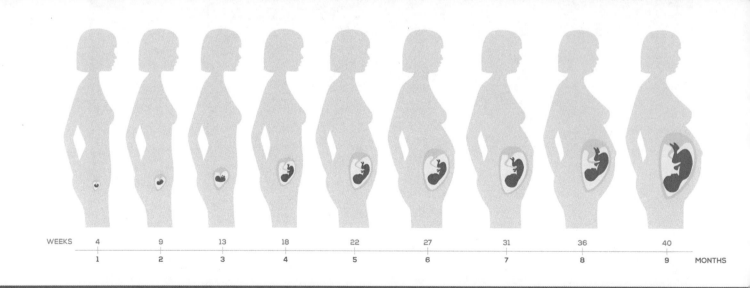

WEEKS	4	9	13	18	22	27	31	36	40	
	1	2	3	4	5	6	7	8	9	MONTHS

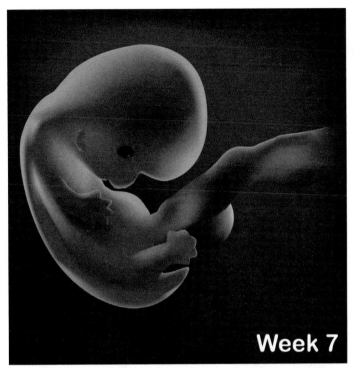

Week 7

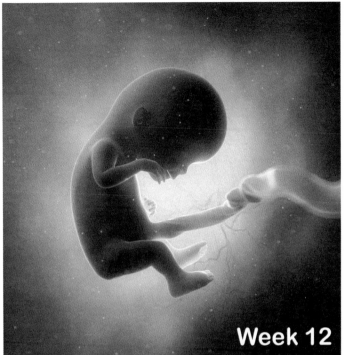

Week 12

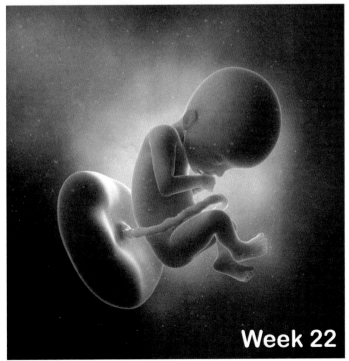

Week 22

Week 38

Every day, you grew bigger
and stronger.

Until, one day...
it was time to leave the womb
and meet your family.

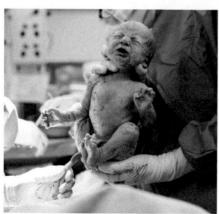
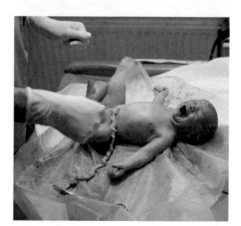

Welcome, Baby!

Made in the USA
Monee, IL
06 June 2022